MW01223636

A New Year, A New You:
52 Strategies for a Happier Life!

By

Dr. Louise T. Lambert, PhD

Text Copyright © 2016 Louise T. Lambert

All Rights Reserved

Disclaimer

The information contained in this book is not intended to replace the advice, diagnosis and treatment recommendations of qualified medical professionals. The author of this book is not liable or otherwise responsible for any reliance by you on any health information or other information found in this book – any such reliance is entirely at your own risk. Never disregard or delay seeking professional medical advice because of information contained in this book.

Contents

Have you ever wondered....?

We have good jobs, holidays, friends, health, and great coffee. Yet, if you're like many people, you're wondering why you're still unhappy. The thing with happiness is that it's slippery, takes work and constant attention, and depends upon much more than our external surroundings and personal circumstances. Happiness comes down to how we see the world, how we interpret what happens to us, how we approach problems, and on what we choose to focus.

Positive psychology, the science of wellbeing, takes happiness as seriously as traditional psychology has historically taken misery. That we know so much about anxiety, depression, and anger shows how seriously psychology has taken its role, but the truth is; we've only just begun looking at happiness in recent years.

We've discovered many interesting things about happiness, one of which is how to get more of it. This book relies upon that empirical research and highlights a number of strategies to increase your happiness over time.

As a psychologist, it's important to rely on evidence-based practices[1] and as a consumer, I hope you agree. Relying on research saves you from wasting effort on things that might make you happy now, but not over time. It also helps you avoid wasting money on unqualified advice like 'Think positively'! If that was all it took, we'd all be happy. Further, relying on strategies that have already been tested on thousands makes it more likely that these tips will work for you too.

Enough... let's get started! This is a book on happiness, after all!

---

[1] *Practitioners familiar with positive psychology will see that the book is organized according to the PERMA pathways: Seligman, M. E. P. (2011). Flourish: A visionary new understanding of happiness and well-being. New York, NY: Free Press.*

Not happy, not depressed...

Happiness is not a good word. For one, it has no definition, and two, it divides the world into two camps, the cheerful unicorns (so annoying!) and miserable sops. In reality, there are many categories, but three are described here: Flourishing, Languishing[2] and the one that needs little introduction, Depressed.

Let's use a thermometer to explain. In the lower temperatures is "Depressed" - the experience of negative feelings and experiences. Feeling anxious, angry, sad, depressed, or discouraged are examples. This doesn't mean that these emotions are bad, they just feel bad. For example, when you fail in a business venture, you feel sullen, embarrassed or angry, but these same emotions can also motivate you to learn from your mistakes, try again, and succeed. The problem with negative emotions is when they persist well beyond the duration of the actual experience or when we create them all by ourselves via our pessimistic, fearful, anxious, or self-conscious thinking. You might spend a lot of time here and it is okay if you do, this book is designed to get you out of this zone.

Near the zeros is "Languishing." It's neither cold nor hot, it's room temperature. In terms of feelings, this means you're not ridiculously happy, but you're not depressed either. It's just feeling blah, sleepy, going through the motions, bored with life, or stuck in neutral. I suspect a lot of us are here, in fact, it's where the majority of people find themselves. They just "are."

Finally, in the positives are "Flourishing" people who experience many positive emotions and experiences. They are not only happier, they function better too. They have good close relationships and are satisfied with work. They have a sense of purpose in life and feel that

---

[2] *Keyes, C. L. M. (2005). Mental illness and/or mental health? Investigating axioms of the complete state model of health. Journal of Consulting and Clinical Psychology, 73, 539–548.*

it's worthwhile. They tend to be in better health and use fewer prescription medications. They even think more effectively than those in the less positive zones of the thermometer. We call them flourishing because they are growing.

Imagine the thermometer goes from -10 (depressed) up to zero for languishing and onwards to +10 for flourishing. Think about where you spend most of your time despite what you might be feeling at this moment and write down your number. The number is your benchmark, so don't worry if it's lower than you'd like.

Most of the time, I am at _____.

What now?

Happiness takes work, but there are a number of strategies to help you get there. Some you will like more than others, but all rely on your effort and consistency. It's a lot like going to the gym; going once won't do anything, but a lifestyle built on physical activity will serve you well over time. Happiness strategies are the same; they need to become part of your lifestyle.

On the other hand, obsessively focusing on happiness and forcing yourself to be happy will be about as effective as only eating carrots in a bid to be healthy, making you tired and resentful. A better way is to try each strategy twice to see how it feels and if it's not your thing, then it's not. There are many strategies and you'll surely find one that fits. Do these about once a week, but no more frequently or happiness will become a job!

But first, why do you want more happiness?

Has anything happened to make you focus on happiness now?

How do you want to be different? Be as specific as you can.

Strategy 1: Is your software working?

Identifying your role

Think about when you are happier. This may be tough as it may have been long ago or just today. Yet, your answers provide clues as to what you need to adjust to make happiness more likely and knowing how you contribute to creating your happiness is vital[3].

When am I generally happier?

What creates that happiness?

[3] *Keyes, C. L. M., Ryff, C. D., & Shmotkin, D. (2002). Optimizing well-being: The empirical encounter of two traditions. Journal of Personality and Social Psychology, 82(6), 1007-1022.*

What role do I play in it? (How do my actions and thoughts make happiness more likely?)

What makes me happy: is it the event or how I am thinking about it?

Strategy 2: What makes me happy?

Identifying happiness

Be creative and write or draw all of the moments, people and/or things that make you happy. (You can do this on a poster board too).

If you came up with even one example, it means your happiness generator works. Happiness doesn't *happen* to you, you create it by interacting with people, situations, activities and your own thoughts. You can win loads of money and a trip around the world but if you're closed to these, they won't matter. You make situations come alive by what you do and how you respond to, and interpret situations.

Ask others...!

Introduce happiness to your social circle by asking people when they are happier. You can do it over coffee, dinner, while driving, at work, or with your kids or parents. Be prepared for laughter, strange looks, and blank answers! Ask many people. Do it now; note their answers.

Person 1	Person 2	Person 3	Person 4
Person 5	Person 6	Person 7	Person 8

Person 9	Person 10	Person 11	Person 12

Did you notice that happier times usually don't involve a new car, shoes or television? OK, maybe a little at the end of a long day with 3 kids! But, normally, answers involve time spent with others, using one's skills, learning, travelling, or engaging one's self in absorbing activity. Other moments might be small like sitting on the beach, cycling, or painting. Happiness is not usually found in objects, even though our society values material things greatly.

Strategy 3: Don't kill it!

Overthinking

You don't do it on purpose; it just sneaks up on you. At first, you innocently review situations, conversations, or other's actions. Then, you ruminate on your feelings, repeat the same phrases, and mentally watch the scenes like a movie. Next thing you know, your good mood is gone. Too much thinking kills happiness[4]!

Of course, not all thinking is bad. Considering problems is how we deal with emotions, find solutions, and make sense of life. It helps us move forward. But, too much thinking becomes overthinking and it's not useful. It's like repeatedly clicking keys on your computer when it's already slow; do it enough and your computer will freeze or crash. Your brain is the same. It can only handle so many things at once and you force-feeding it with repeated thoughts, is not helpful.

What does your overthinking sound like?

---

[4] *Lyubomirsky, S., & Tkach, C. (2003). The consequences of dysphoric rumination. In C. Papageorgiou & A. Wells (Eds.), Rumination: Nature, theory, and treatment of negative thinking in depression (pp. 21-41). Chichester, UK: John Wiley & Sons.*

When do you know you've gone too far?

What does it affect (i.e., other relationships, health, sleep, etc.)?

Overthinking strengthens the emotions you're trying to get rid of; like a headache, the more you focus on it, the more intense it becomes. Overthinking also leads to confusion about which direction to take and moves us further away from solutions. The more we do it, the more it becomes a habit. Overthinking also stops us from being in the moment, such that something good might be occurring, but we are too deep in thought and miss it. How do you minimize or stop overthinking? Think of times you've overcome it, even for a few minutes, what did you do?

Overthinking affects positives too; when we over-analyze them, they lose their mystery and delight. Do you overthink positives? What happens to your joy as a result?

Here are ways to limit overthinking. Consider how they might work for you and add your ideas. Once you control your overthinking, there will be more space for positive emotions and experiences.

Idea 1: Do something physical: walk, run, play squash, walk stairs, stretch. Physical efforts force you to breath, interrupt your thinking, and clear your mind. How would this work for me?

Idea 2: Write it. But use order. What's the exact problem? What's my role in it? What can I do to solve it (even if I don't want to)? When? How? How can I prevent it next time? How would this work for me?

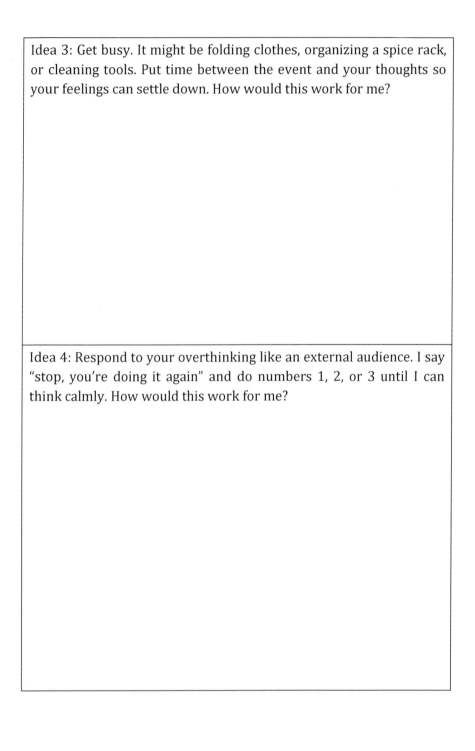

Idea 3: Get busy. It might be folding clothes, organizing a spice rack, or cleaning tools. Put time between the event and your thoughts so your feelings can settle down. How would this work for me?

Idea 4: Respond to your overthinking like an external audience. I say "stop, you're doing it again" and do numbers 1, 2, or 3 until I can think calmly. How would this work for me?

Idea 5: Purposefully plan the day by removing the need to overthink. This will help put order to what you do, limit unnecessary decision making and perhaps prevent issues. How would this work for me?

Other ideas to combat overthinking:

Strategy 4: Attach your head to your feet!

Mindfulness

You may have heard about mindfulness[5] and there are many ways to understand it. Here's my favorite: Keep your head attached to your feet! Let me explain...

You're reading this book; yet, your thoughts might be elsewhere. Your head has disconnected and it's travelling to the past thinking of events from 2009. The more you think, the worse you feel and other memories pop up too. You've read the last three sentences repeatedly, but retained nothing.

At other times, your head goes the other way and worries about things it thinks are coming but haven't. Before you know it, you're in 2019 and anxious. You've lost connection to now. Your feet are here but they are useless because your head is not. Sound familiar?

How much time do you spend being disconnected from your immediate reality?

---

[5] *Brown, K. W., Ryan, R. M., & Creswell, J. D. (2007). Addressing fundamental questions about mindfulness. Psychological Inquiry, 18(4), 272-281.*

How does it help?

How is it not helpful?

When we disconnect, we are mindless. We do not focus on the immediate present, but focus inward and create an internal story that is not always real. We create much of our own stress by mentally replaying negative events that are long gone. It's hard to stay in the present where most often not much is happening, but we need to train our minds to do that more frequently.

I have been through some terrible things in my life, some of which actually happened.

Mark Twain (1835 - 1910)

Can you drive a car?

Think of mindfulness as the ability to keep a car on the road and not losing control and driving over curbs and through stop signs. So, only if you can keep a car on the road can you allow yourself to think of the past and future (a little worry is okay, it helps us plan), and only if you can focus on the positive or perhaps the negatives if there is a purpose and in small doses. If you can't, sorry, hand over the keys and get more practice! Here's how.

Notice the external

Sitting here now, at this time, notice what's happening around you. What do you hear? A car driving by, neighbors, a bird, the hum of lights, air conditioner, silence? What do you smell? Dust, fragrance, laundry soap? What do you see? A door, chair, blanket, the street? What do you feel against you? A pillow, couch, bench, sand, or grass? While focused on these things, here and now - are you okay?

Maybe you've got a toothache that made you say no, but generally people say yes when they reflect on the immediate moment. We need to be in the present to not get stuck in the past or future and create turmoil for nothing. There are enough hazards in life; you don't need to create more on your own.

When you notice that you've travelled to the past for no reason or are imagining future events that may happen but probably won't, return to the present by asking these questions. Practice them now.

What can I see?
What can I smell?
What can I touch?
What can I physically feel against/on me?
What can I hear?
What can I taste?

Will mindfulness make you happy? No. But, we need to clear some mental space to give happiness a chance. You can't feel happy if you're busy worrying or being sad. Mindfulness only takes a few seconds and no one will notice what you're up to.

Practice mindfulness this week and write about it in the next section. Don't move ahead until you do, otherwise you'll just be reading about happiness and not actually living it. See you in a few days.

Driving school practice!
This week, try mindfulness three times and write about it. Remember not to get frustrated; you'll only cause overthinking! And by the way, it likely won't work the first time. The second time you'll forget and the third will happen for 10 seconds. Be patient, happiness involves retraining the brain like learning a new language.

Attempt 1: Date, time and what happened:

Attempt 2: Date, time and what happened:

Attempt 3: Date, time and what happened:

If you were successful, what was the result of using mindfulness?

What works well and what makes mindfulness difficult?

Strategy 5: Less is best.

Satisfice

Most of us typically don't have this problem, but the following example illustrates the difficulties of making choices and how these can impact our happiness.

Let's say you want to get married and your friends, mother, and aunts start interviewing potential mates. Tall, short, toned, rich, intelligent, well-travelled and interesting partners; how to choose? Each is as good as the next and every choice made means one is rejected. You finally choose. They're great, but knowing there were other good options makes you feel as though you might have made a mistake even though nothing says you did.

This is called the Baskin Robbins effect (like the ice cream), where too many options make us unhappy because we have knowledge of what we could have had, but didn't choose. So, how should we make decisions? People tend to either satisfice or maximize[6].

Happier people use *satisficing*, they set minimum standards for what they need to be happy, i.e., tall, funny, kind, and once they reach it, decide. By limiting their options, they reach 'good enough' and make it work thereafter. In contrast, less happy people *maximize,* trying to make a perfect decision and creating endless options that are time consuming and overwhelming. Maximizing also makes comparisons more likely guaranteeing that we find something better and become unhappy as a result.

---

[6] *Schwartz, B. (2000). Self-determination: The tyranny of freedom. American Psychologist, 55(1), 79-88.*

Are you a satisficer or maximizer? How well do these work for you?

Think of a decision you are facing and your minimum standards so that you know when to stop looking. It might be a new job, house, or next holiday. Apply satisficing more often and see what happens.

I need _____, _____, _____, to be happy in _____.

You can have more than three standards, but the more you have, the longer you spend without the situation you want.

Strategy 6: Care a little less.

Comparisons

Miriam got a work promotion! Hana is pleased for Miriam and thinks of how she can celebrate, maybe take her to lunch. In contrast, Bill congratulates Miriam, but wonders why he didn't get a promotion? He is just as good and considers this unfair. He was having a good day, but ruined it by comparing himself to Miriam.

Measuring our success against that of others is a recipe for feeling bad because there is always someone doing better, moving faster, or with a different situation. Yet, happy people care less about the success of others in the sense that they do not use the good news of others to decide whether their own achievements are worthwhile[7]. They use their own standards for that.

Do you compare yourself to others? How does it make you feel?

[7] Abbe, A., Tkach, C., & Lyubomirsky, S. (2003). The art of living by dispositionally happy people. *Journal of Happiness Studies, 4*, 385-404.

What are the costs to doing it even if there are some positives to it?

Might you need to change these mental comparisons? What can you do, think of, or tell yourself instead?

Strategy 7: It's all in where you look.

Find the positive

Carl and Mark got in a car accident. They suffered broken bones and had to take time off work. Yet, how each responded was interesting. Carl got depressed and thought about how much worse it could have been. He was upset at having to go for physiotherapy and became angry with people who tried to help. Mark was also shaken by the event, but vowed to become physically stronger and looked forward to going to physiotherapy as until then, he hadn't been taking care of himself. And even though he was off work, he arranged to do a little from home, enough to keep him busy. He invited a friend every day to keep him company too. Instead of being defeated, he took it in stride.

Happier people look for the good in the bad and do it on purpose[8] because it's neither easy, nor obvious to find the good in a car accident. In case you're wondering, happy people are sad when bad things happen and respond like everyone else, but they force themselves to look for positives as a way to move forward.

---

[8] *Abbe, A., Tkach, C., & Lyubomirsky, S. (2003). The art of living by dispositionally happy people. Journal of Happiness Studies, 4, 385-404. Lyubomirsky, S., & Tucker, K. L. (1998). Implications of individual differences in subjective happiness for perceiving, interpreting, and thinking about life events. Motivation and Emotion, 22, 155-186.*

Are you easily defeated or do you give yourself permission to feel bad for a time and then focus on the positives to move ahead?

If you're like Carl, how can you focus on the positives? Try it now, is there something you could think about differently to help you move forward?

Strategy 8: Don't blame me!

Focus in, not out

Years ago, a study[9] was conducted with people who'd won a lot of money and others who'd become paraplegics. At first, the winners were happy spending money, but three months on, their happiness levels returned to normal. In fact, the money made it harder for them to like the things they used to. They assumed that with money, life would be full of excitement, but soon realized that you still have to exercise, talk with your spouse, and do something productive.

The individuals who became paraplegics had to make tough adjustments. They worried about things like relationships, getting around physically, work prospects and daily living. At three months, their happiness levels were still low, but by six months, they were almost back to normal. It took them longer to adapt, but the fact that they did says we adapt to negative events too.

What does this mean? Circumstances matter little over time because we get used to them[10] and *adapt[11]*; thus, things like not getting the job you want, are not ideal events to blame for why you are unhappy.

Yet, adaptation is bad for good events as it means you'll get used to positive changes quickly (even faster when changes are superficial), and you'll have to keep refreshing those challenges or opportunities over time so that the emotional impact remains. On the other hand, adaptation is good for bad events and means that if you can hang on long enough, the emotional sting of bad events will eventually fade.

---

[9] Brickman, P., Coates, D., & Janoff-Bulman, R. (1978). Lottery winners and accident victims: Is happiness relative? Journal of Personality and Social Psychology, 36, 917-927.
[10] Lyubomirsky, S., Sheldon, K. M., & Schkade, D. (2005). Pursuing happiness: The architecture of sustainable change. Review of General Psychology, 9(2), 111-131.
[11] Lyubomirsky, S. (2011). Hedonic adaptation to positive and negative experiences. In S. Folkman (Ed.), Oxford handbook of stress, health, and coping (pp. 200-224). New York, NY: Oxford University Press.

Do you blame circumstances for your unhappiness? Does it work?

Do you look to external events to make you happy? Does it work?

How long does it take you to adapt to the good? What can you do so that the effect of good things lasts longer?

Strategy 9: Spend it right!

Choose experience

Do you think money leads to happiness? You're sort of right.

If you can't meet basic needs like food, clothing, and housing, money will for sure make you happier. But, beyond that, it doesn't add much to happiness because we adapt to money and in the face of more, only find additional ways to spend it[12]. However, if you can meet your needs, how you spend money becomes important.

Investing in experience (like going on holiday), as opposed to investing in objects (like shoes) is more effective in generating happiness[13] as material goods can be lost, broken, or surpassed by newer models. Experiences are also unpredictable, leaving plenty of room for random people, conversations, unexpected events and surprise friends. Objects on the other hand are predictable; they do what they are meant to do and beyond their function, do little else. If you link happiness to things, you might even begin to think objects define you. Don't get me wrong, having money isn't bad; but, what you do with it indeed matters to your happiness.

---

[12] *Diener, E., & Biswas-Diener, R. (2002). Will money increase subjective well-being? A literature review and guide to needed research. Social Indicators Research, 57, 119-169.*
[13] *Van Boven, L. (2005). Experientialism, materialism, and the pursuit of happiness. Review of General Psychology, 9, 132-142; Van Boven, L., & Gilovich, T. (2003). To do or to have? That is the question. Journal of Personality and Social Psychology, 85(6), 1193-1202.*

Whether you have a lot or a little doesn't matter, are you more focused on experiences or objects? Which has been more meaningful in the past? Which has led to growth and positive experiences?

Can you plan an experience (preferably a fun or meaningful one) with the money you would have used for an object? What can you do? With whom will you share the experience?

Strategy 10: Go ahead, 'inst'-it!

Purposeful documentation

We have much good in our lives but due to adaptation, the fact that we get used to good things, we fail to see it. This activity[14] will help you look at your life with new eyes.

Taking photos, whether we go back and look at them or not, forces us to stop and notice details that we take for granted and consider the significance of what we see. Photos also help us imprint scenes to memory. Yet, we tend to only do this on holiday; why not every day?

Pick a morning, afternoon, or evening and experience your usual surroundings like a tourist. Notice plant growth, interesting architectural angles, scenery, meals, movement, birds, or your regular morning walk. Force yourself to find and appreciate something new. Collect your photos and save them in a folder. You can even make a video. Every month, pick a slice of time and document it. You'll enjoy the present more and build memories for later. If you have kids, have them join you in the activity and make a folder for themselves or as a family.

Report on how it went here; but for now, decide on which day you will do it.

Where will you go?

With who?

---

[14] *Kurtz, J. L., & Lyubomirsky, S. (2013). Using mindful photography to increase positive emotion and appreciation. In J. F. Froh & A. C. Parks (Eds.), Activities for teaching positive psychology: A guide for instructors (pp. 133-136). Washington, DC: APA.*

How did this activity work for you?

Strategy 11: It's better than you think!

3 good things

Naming three good things is a way to find and focus on the positives. Studies[15] show that if you take time to find three good things every day, it can keep depression at bay. You can write about it each day in a happiness journal too; it just can't be the same three things each day! You can even use this as a subject of dinner conversation with your partner, children, or friends.

Sometimes people can't find good things. In that case, focus on the bad events that could have happened but didn't. For instance, I did not experience a hurricane, drought, or civil war today. People experience these things all the time. Today, you did not. Sometimes, the absence of a negative is all you'll get. It counts too.

Note your three good things for today and then continue finding three good things every day for the week.

Today: 3 good things...

---

[15] *Seligman, M. P., Steen, T. A., Park, N., & Peterson, C. (2005). Positive psychology progress. American Psychologist, 60(5), 410-421.*

Day 2:

Day 3:

Day 4:

Day 5:

Day 6:

Day 7:

What was it like to do this activity? What did you learn?

Strategy 12: Take a vacation, now!

Revitalization

Are you counting the days until your next holiday? Holidays are great; but, we seem to have missed the point of them. For one, we have the idea that we can only have a holiday after and only if we've worked hard. It's considered a reward. And yet, the purpose of a holiday is to take a break from the normal[16], be exposed to new people, ideas, scenery, and foods. In fact, you think nothing of walking into neighborhoods, ducking into random stores, asking strangers where to eat, and visiting every museum on the map! The novelty is refreshing, inspiring, and motivating. So, wouldn't it make more sense to take holidays more often?

By reorganizing the day and taking 15 minutes of "holiday," there are many things we can do to get the same benefits as a proper holiday, like…

Drive to a nearby park and walk for five minutes.
Read a magazine on a park bench listening to birds.
Go into that art gallery, instead of just looking at it.
Have your coffee in a different café across town.
Walk in a different neighborhood.
Take a different road to work even if it's longer to see what's new.
Go to your local museum(s).
Attend a book reading. If it's boring, leave.
Watch the sunrise – you'd do it in Italy, why not at home?
Walk on the beach without your phone.

Aim to have a daily 'vacation' for the next three days or more. See what difference it makes to your day, productivity, and mood and decide if it's something you can do more often.

---

[16] *Sonnentag, S., & Fritz, C. (2015). Recovery from job stress. Journal of Organizational Behavior, 36, S76–S103.*

My 10 mini-holiday ideas for the next 3 days:

The secret's out!

Defining happiness

In positive psychology, a formal definition of happiness does not yet exist in the same way it does for depression. Nonetheless, one theory states that happiness is the experience of positive emotions gained from gratifications, things that give instant positivity like receiving a hug from a child, or smelling freshly baked bread. But first, list as many positive emotions as you can here:

That's often tough because we pay little attention to positive emotions; but, according to the broaden and build model[17], you get an injection of happiness any time you experience one. Thus, with happiness defined as the occurrence of any positive emotion, happiness is far easier to identify and create. Think of it like this: say we have a scale of 1 to 10 and happiness is a 10. This sets the bar high to start and means that we only accept happiness as the times when there are disco balls, confetti and rainbows. I don't know about you, but if this is happiness, I'm miserable!

---

[17] *Fredrickson, B. L. (2006). The broaden and build theory of positive emotions. In M. Csikszentmihalyi & I. S. Csikszentmihalyi (Eds.), A life worth living: Contributions to positive psychology (pp. 85-103). New York: Oxford University Press; Fredrickson, B. L., & Joiner, T. (2002). Positive emotions trigger upward spirals toward emotional well-being. Psychological Science, 13, 172-175.*

It does not mean that 10's don't occur, they do and might be the day you get married (or divorced!), have a baby, or graduate from university. Most people will have less than a handful of 10's — that's why they are special, they are rare and if we had many, we wouldn't appreciate them as much. What about the moments below 10? We often overlook them, but happiness is also the 1s, 3s, and 5s of life. When we change the definition of happiness, the frequency with which we experience it increases. In other words, you're likely happier than you realized.

How do you feel about the new definition of happiness? Is it disappointing? Is it a relief?

Positive emotions

Inspiration, love, gratitude, curiosity, interest, vitality, joy, hope, pride, amusement, serenity, and awe are a few positive emotions. Here is a list that will help you in the next activities.

Pleasure tells us that an activity is rewarding; yet, not all pleasures are good like smoking. But, when beneficial, pleasures can reduce stress, aid coping, encourage sociability, and impact health positively[18]. Pleasures can be instantly felt holding a child's hand, savoring hot chocolate, listening to music, or running.

Vitality is the experience of feeling alive and happens when you are physically fit and psychologically well and includes a sense of purpose and meaning[19]. It's related to physical health, agency (feeling like you can make things happen) and self-actualization (reaching goals and becoming our best selves).

Curiosity is when we recognize something of interest and pursue it[20] by generating new behavior, focusing our attention, exploring new things and changing our views as a result.

Inspiration consists of transcendence, meaning that we attend to something bigger than our usual life concerns; evocation, meaning inspiration happens and cannot be planned; and motivation, a desire to do something[21].

---

[18] Veenhoven, R. (2003). Hedonism and happiness. Journal of Happiness Studies, 4, 437-457.

[19] Ryan, R. M., & Bernstein, J. H. (2004). Vitality: Zest, enthusiasm, vigor, energy. In C. Peterson & M. E. P. Seligman (Eds.), Character strengths and virtues: A handbook and classification (pp. 273-289). Oxford: Oxford University Press.

[20] Kashdan, T. B. (2004). Curiosity. In C. Peterson and M. E. P. Seligman (Eds.), Character strengths and virtues: A handbook and classification (pp.125-141). New York: Oxford University Press/Washington, DC, American Psychological Association.

[21] Thrash, T. M., & Elliot, A. J. (2004). Inspiration: Core characteristics, component processes, antecedents, and function. Journal of Personality and Social Psychology, 87(6), 957-973.

Awe[22] involves anything experienced as larger than one's self, as well as the mental changes that occur in response to what was unknown until then. To awe, we respond with humility. Closely related is *elevation*[23], an emotion felt as a result of witnessing kind and selfless acts. It is moving, uplifting and triggers us to be more pro-social as we feel a desire to help, love, and be close to others.

Gratitude is the awareness of others goodness directed at us[24]. By recognizing that positive events are due to the kindness of others, we see ourselves as receivers of generosity and as worthwhile people.

Optimism involves thoughts, feelings, and actions that help us move ahead with challenge[25]. It may be a form of self-deception that motivates us to close the gap between reality and outcomes, but also a sense that life will bring good things. *Hope* involves images of the actions required to achieve goals[26]. High-hope people think of many goal pathways and believe in their ability to reach them.

Pride is experienced when we consider success the result of our own efforts[27]. It can extend to others, like when watching the Olympics, a child's poetry competition, or friend's graduation. Pride can signal you've done something good and is a result of positive living.

---

[22] *Haidt, J., & Seder, P. (2009) Admiration and Awe. Entry for the Oxford Companion to Affective Science (pp. 4-5). New York: Oxford University Press.*

[23] *Algoe, S., & Haidt, J., (2009). Witnessing excellence in action: The other-praising emotions of elevation, admiration, and gratitude. Journal of Positive Psychology, 4, 105-127.*

[24] *Emmons, R. A., & Mishra, A. (2012). Why gratitude enhances well-being: What we know, what we need to know. In Sheldon, K., Kashdan, T., & Steger, M. F. (Eds.) Designing the future of positive psychology: Taking stock and moving forward (pp. 248-262). New York: Oxford University Press.*

[25] *Peterson, C. (2000). The future of optimism. American Psychologist, 55(1), 44-55.*

[26] *Snyder, C. R. (2002). Hope theory: Rainbows of the mind. Psychological Inquiry, 13, 249-275.*

[27] *Tracy, J. L., Weidman, A. C., Cheng, J. T., & Martens, J. P. (2014). Pride: The fundamental emotion of success, power, and status. In M. M. Tugade, M. N. Shiota, & L. D. Kirby (Eds.), Handbook of positive emotion (pp. 294-310). New York: Guildford Press.*

It's good to recognize positive emotions so that you can identify them when they occur. Be mindful though as positive emotions are light and short-lived. Catch them when they arise and savor them.

When I experience positive emotions, how does my approach to life change?

How would others say I am different under the influence of positive emotions? What do they notice?

Strategy 13: Let the count begin!

The positivity ratio

While pleasures are easy to get, they are not enough to assure happiness over time. This is due to the fact that positive emotions weigh little and disappear quickly. In fact, compared to negative emotions, we need three to offset one negative emotion[28]. Thus, we should be on the lookout for positive emotions.

Yet, notice there is room for negative emotion (it's three to one, not three to none), so you don't need to remove them, only increase the positive ones to increase the gap between them. Can you track your positivity ratio? Think of today and recall how many positive emotions you've experienced compared to the negative so far.

_____ : _____

positive emotions   negative emotions

Tracking your ratio during the day can help you notice how much time you spend in the negative. The aim is to increase the number on the left, so don't worry too much about the number on the right. Do this a few days in a row to see if you are in the languishing (no growth) or flourishing zone.

Next, see how much time you spend in the experience of positive emotion by considering your activities and filling in the chart below. Be honest in considering whether the activity brings you positive emotion because of the expectation that it should, or whether it truthfully does. How many times have you gone to an expensive, "to die for" restaurant that was overpriced, average and uninteresting,

---

[28] *Practitioners should know about the debate surrounding the 3:1 ratio. Read the original article: Fredrickson, B. L., & Losada, M. (2005). Positive affect and the complex dynamics of human flourishing. American Psychologist, 60(7), 678-686. Read the critique of the ratio: Brown, N. J. L., Sokal, A. D., & Friedman, H. L. (2013). The complex dynamics of wishful thinking: The critical positivity ratio. American Psychologist, 68, 801–813.*

but that everyone pretended to love? You might have said it was great to fit in, but your experiencing self knew far better[29].

The chart in the next activity will help you decide what is pleasurable and what you might do more often. And if you're like some people, it might be simply reading a book. Don't be ashamed of what you like. Track what makes you feel good for a few days to get an idea of what fits you versus what is supposed to fit you.

[29] Dolan, P. (2015). Happiness by design: Change what you do, not how you think. USA: Plume Books.

Strategy 14: Positive emotion generators

Day	Before work	Morning	Afternoon	Evening

My best activities that consistently bring in positive emotions:

Are there things you experience positively but evaluate negatively? For example, I get pleasure from housework, but I'm not supposed to, so I don't consider it a positive event.

Are there activities you evaluate positively (i.e., fancy restaurant), but don't in fact experience positively?

What might you do differently as a result of this charting activity?

Strategy 15: Remember when....?

Positive reminiscing

This activity is useful when you have nothing to feel good about. After all, not every day is great; some are bad and others neutral.

Mark had a revelation when he did this exercise. He chose to recollect his wedding day which took place in the 1970's. It was in the church and he was at the altar waiting for his bride. He was wearing white pleather shoes, the kind that make your feet sweat. His suit was white polyester and he had a blue blouse underneath with a frilly opening. He even described his perm! After a few moments, his bride began to come down the aisle and he thought he was going to faint because he was so nervous. He remembered her huge dress, curly tendrils on each side of her head, and blue eye-shadow...he recalled thinking "Angie is the love of my life! I can't think of anywhere else I would rather be than here." He got tearful and broken voiced as he told us and we did too. But, what came next was profound. "We divorced about two years later, but it doesn't take away from the fact that I was happy that day. Since then, I haven't felt that sort of happiness, ever. I'm thankful to know what that felt like, because some people have never felt love like that..."

How something ends does not take away from the fact that it was.

This week, think and write about your positive experiences[30]. Describe the scene and the feelings of that moment. Positive moments do not last long. You'll only have a few lines, but you'll re-experience and reap the benefits of that experience once more. Make sure to only write about the time itself, not what came later or how it disappeared or ended badly. Take your time. When done, consider how you feel. Did your ratio increase? Share your memory with someone or write a memory for each of the positive emotions over several days or weeks. The more you do, the more positivity becomes a habit.

[30] Bryant, F. B., Smart, C. M., & King, S. P. (2005). Using the past to enhance the present: Boosting happiness through positive reminiscence. Journal of Happiness Studies, 6, 227-260.

Strategy 16: Slow down with that latte!

Savoring

I can drown my latte in a matter of minutes while scrolling on my iPhone or I can focus on its taste, texture, and smell and actually enjoy it. While I love lattes, sometimes I multitask and ignore its experience as a result. What I should be doing is savoring, noticing the steam rise in the cup, imbibe the caramel and strong smell of coffee, and let the creaminess melt in my mouth! I'm doing it anyways, why not enjoy it?

Savoring[31] involves appreciating and extending positive experiences. By taking in the details of what we see, hear, smell, taste, and feel, we build memories to recollect later. We can savor a walk in the park, food, music, or crossing things off a to-do list. It takes no extra time or effort; savoring only requires you to notice what already exists.

Savor at least three moments today and then again over the week by attending to pleasure and being present in your experiences instead of focusing outside watching traffic or ruminating on negative thoughts. We are surrounded by moments of pleasure and goodness all day long, but must attend to them in order to benefit.

---

[31] *Bryant, F. B., & Veroff, J. (2006). Savoring: A new model of positive experience. Mahwah, NJ: Erlbaum.*

What do you currently savor? What can you savor more closely?
Think of three more things from your typical routine to savor more.

What were my savoring moments?

    1.

    2.

    3.

Strategy 17: Go for gold!

Optimism

People think optimism is being silly, naïve, and blind to the realities of life, but so is being cautious, skeptical, and mistrusting! Optimism is not about pretending reality doesn't exist; it is about choosing a mindset for success[32].

Imagine you're going for an interview. You doubt it will work out. This low mood saps your energy, makes you seem glum, and promotes overthinking and self-doubt to the point where you respond to questions poorly. You give the impression that you couldn't be bothered. Surprise, you don't get it! Not because you couldn't have, but because your pessimism caused you to act and think in a way that brought out the worst in you.

Try again.

You're hopeful, expectant that something good will come from this and as a result, put your best foot forward by smiling and being the witty charmer you are. You're open to conversation, attentive and conscious of your strengths. Whether the job works out or not isn't the point, it's that optimism promotes success by changing your behavior and thoughts, which in turn, increase the chance of success.

---

[32] *Shapira, L. B., & Mongrain, M. (2010). The benefits of self-compassion and optimism exercises for individuals vulnerable to depression. Journal of Positive Psychology, 5, 377–389.*

Think of a situation you are facing (or will be) and develop three optimistic beliefs and/or actions like in the situation above. You may have a quote or saying to remind you that the future will be brighter, or a song to put you in a good mood. If there is no current negative situation, do not create one! One will come along soon enough, so don't go get it. Instead, note how you use optimism now and see if you can improve it for the purpose of getting the best from yourself.

Strategy 18: Plan it.

Purposeful action

How many of you have had a great day from morning to finish where everything you wanted, as well as everyone you liked appeared in some way and you had a great positive mindset to enjoy it all? It's rare, right? And a lot depends on what is happening around us like school or work demands, other people's moods, traffic, family, etc. But, let's pretend for a moment that none of these had an impact on the day, your mood or thoughts. They were powerless.

Design such a day[33] for yourself. Regardless of whether you have problems, frustrations, or worries, none of these have an impact. It really is going to be a fantastic day. Go ahead and plan it by asking yourself these questions: What would I wear? What would I listen to or do on the way to work or school? What would I eat? Who would I speak to? How would I make it special for someone else? How would I treat myself, maybe a latte on a park bench with a friend laughing at funny videos? Would I go bowling? Paint? Take a boat ride? Call my grandfather? Take him with me on the boat ride?

Plan a great day and make it as special as you can as though it was your birthday! Note it on the next page. And remember, even if something bad happens, unless it's tragic, you can deal with it later or choose not to worry about it. Most things aren't that important, we just make them so.

---

[33] *Dunn, D. S., Beard, B. M., & Fisher, D. J. (2011). On happiness: Introducing students to positive psychology. In R. Miller, E. Balcetis, S. R. Burns, D. B. Daniel, B. K. Saville, & W. D. Woody (Eds.), Promoting student engagement (Vol. 2, pp. 207–216). Retrieved from Society for the Teaching of Psychology Web site: http://teachpsych.org/resources/ebooks/pse2011/index.php*

Spectator or Player?

There are more ways to be happy and these involve the attachments we have to the activities in which we spend a lot of time and feel are important, which can include playing the piano, soccer, writing a novel, or painting. Typically, these use our talents and skills, physical and mental effort, as well as our energy and excitement. When we commit and become good at them, we are further rewarded with a state of flow, a feeling of absorption, as well as greater life meaning. We become better at those skills and talents and become better versions of ourselves by using them. Yet, the key is time, not being fearful of hard work, and sticking with activities long enough to see results. Thus, these activities aren't done once, but repeatedly. As Aristotle said, excellence is found in the habits we have.

List the activities in which you spend a lot of time outside of work and family that use your strengths, effort, and energy, and that you've been doing for some time. What are they?

Why hard is better.

These days, we have lives of great convenience; maids, drive-through banks, McDonald's and dry cleaning! Even if you'd like to do hard work, it becomes harder to do as there are so many devices to make it easy. As a result, it can be tough to exert effort, move, and challenge ourselves. The tragedy is that we lose opportunities to develop our skills and talents – ourselves - and build excellence as a result. Doing easy stuff doesn't exercise the body, mind, or our personalities, but hard stuff does.

We also have the idea that anything unrelated to work, family, or friends is a waste. For instance, have your parents ever told you that sports are for kids, art is for school, music is for bohemians?! Nonsense! These activities are where we learn to be great. Take sports, it's where we use our strengths to cooperate, accept losses, discipline ourselves, learn about and control our bodies through good nutrition and sleep, surpass mental limits, and strive with our opponents towards excellence. Where else do we practice that?

Think about the times you did something tough. How did it help you grow? What skills did you use? What did you learn and how did you feel about yourself after you did it? Do easy things teach you this?

I know you've dreamed of doing something tough. Maybe you've never shared it with others because it seemed too hard. Go on, write it here. If your effort, talents, zest, and time were guaranteed, what's something difficult you'd do? Maybe climb Mount Everest, play the saxophone, speak Mandarin? Start by writing what comes to mind and then you can go over it with a different colored pen and make some suggestions to get yourself started. You don't have to do this amazing thing, but write out as many steps as possible as to how you could do it. Let it simmer and see how you feel in a few days.

Strategy 19: Plan it: Wishing isn't enough!

Goal setting

Harry wants to improve his fitness, but has done nothing for 9 years. He got on a treadmill and tried to run. He took off fast and lasted 27 seconds! He was embarrassed and went home. Sound familiar? It's not enough for Harry to believe he can do something; he needs a plan to get there and goals[34] help us to do that.

Goals provide us with direction and help us organize and master our time as well as achieve a sense of control. With goals, we have a reason to get up in the morning. Goals also pull us towards the future and give us a space in which to retreat when times are tough.

How to set goals? Let's go back to Harry. First, he needs to change his expectations. He has been sitting for years. It's not going to happen in 27 seconds! All good things take time; yet, he can realize small gains quickly if he plans them right. He can consider doing a slow jog or a fast walk for 30 seconds and see how he feels. If it's easy, he can do another 30 seconds and then add 30 second walking intervals to catch his breath until he reaches 5 minutes. If this is still too much, he can do 30 seconds, rest for 1 minute, do another 30 and stop.

The point is to start from your current level (even if it's zero) and build targets by adding small increments and tracking your success over time. You can track your success by jotting down your activity in terms of minutes, intervals, weights, speed, score, or whatever it is you are doing. Progress is motivating.

Further, goals must be enjoyable otherwise you'll quit. Seems simple; yet, you'd be surprised at how many people make it a goal to go the gym which they hate, when swimming or salsa dancing would suit

---

[34] *Lutz, R., Karoly, P., & Okun, M. (2008). The why and the how of goal pursuit: Self-determination, goal process cognition, and participation in physical exercise. Psychology of Sport and Exercise, 9, 559–575.*

them better. Further, select goals to approach rather than avoid. An example is choosing to eat an extra serving of vegetables a day instead of not eating junk food. Not doing something keeps you in a state of wanting and it's miserable. Set small goals that can be reached within a week. If it's too big, break it down until you reach it and go upwards from there.

Finally, your goal should be realistic, sustainable over time, and personal to you versus what others think you must do. If you don't engage in physical activity, going for a daily 5 minute walk might be enough until it becomes a habit and then you can add time as you go. For others, this might be too little and your goal may be to run an hour. Choose what works for you.

Below, choose two medium term goals and break them into small steps. Then, outline those smaller steps starting from this week onwards. It's okay to adjust the timeline as you go, but don't pick something so far into the future that you'll forget or burnout on the way. And remember that a good goal uses your skills and talents and doesn't contribute to worse outcomes, like watching more television! An example of a goal might include becoming fluent enough in Italian to travel there by spring, or playing a song on the piano by winter.

Goal Number 1 Steps:

1.

2.

3.

Goal Number 2 Steps:

1.

2.

3.

What's my first step – starting today – to begin reaching this goal?

How will I deal with self-defeating thoughts that stop me from attaining my goals?

Is there anything else I need to get started? What else might help me? Who else might help me?

We're programmed to get bored!

When Harry first started running, ouf!, it was hard; he could barely do a minute. But, within several weeks, he got better and reached 45 minutes. Yet, strangely, he also got bored and eventually quit as it became a chore.

Remember adaptation, the habituation we experience to both negative and positive events? Another way to understand adaptation relates to skills. Harry adapted because he became good at running. When you become good at something, adaptation is natural. It means there is nothing left to learn, you've done it! Hurrah! Boredom[35] is a signal for you to challenge yourself again for continued growth.

Have you adapted to your activities? Which ones? What got boring?

Think of activities you've done in the past (or now) that you really liked but stopped because they got boring. Which did you once like?

---

[35] *Csikszentmihalyi, M. (2000). Beyond boredom and anxiety. San Francisco: Jossey Bass. (Original work published in 1975)*

Which might you like to start up again? Can you recall what you liked about the activity? What made it pleasurable? Recall good moments about it.

Strategy 20: Stop the boredom!

Prevent adaptation

Here's what you and Harry can do to push back against adaptation[36].

1. Expect it. You may love chocolate, but you'd get bored eating it every day. We adapt to everything. It's normal.
2. Make it harder. Harry can increase his incline, speed up, or race against the clock. He can even sign up for long races.
3. Use variety. He can run outside, in a pool, do a slow but steep day and alternate with a fast downhill day. He can race against friends, or alternate with weights or cycling. He can change music and listen to the radio instead, or run in new areas with new people.
4. Change the frequency or timing. He can run less, maybe twice a week, so he can miss it. He can change the time at which he runs, or run more than once a day but with shorter times.

Adaptation is important to know about as many activities that are good for us and help us grow can be wasted for this reason. If you start to get bored, it's not a sign to stop or that the activity isn't for you, it means you're getting really good at it and you need to manage your pathway to excellence otherwise.

---

[36] *Lyubomirsky, S. (2011). Hedonic adaptation to positive and negative experiences. In S. Folkman (Ed.), Oxford handbook of stress, health, and coping (pp. 200–224). New York, NY: Oxford University Press.*

Thinking of past activities you've stopped or current ones that are threatening you with adaptation, what can you do to prevent adaptation? Write your anti-boredom plan here.

Strategy 21: Mix it up!

Variety

Just like you used variety to combat adaptation, you can also use variety to put spice in your life! This is especially needed when we're stressed and tired and keep returning to the same things and events to refresh us. Constantly watching Netflix, even if an initial source of happiness gets dull after a while and stops having the desired effect; thus, knowing how to refresh ourselves effectively is important for our mood, view on life, and productivity throughout the day.

One of the best ways to recharge is to do something you've never done before[37] so you're forced to learn, pay attention, and develop new skills that keep you sharp. Plus, it's a good way to have fun and meet people you normally wouldn't. New things also build memories for the future. Examples of novelty in our activities might be trying badminton, taking a painting lesson, or going fishing and holding a real fish! You might even try a ballroom dancing lesson, hula hooping, or attend a wine tasting event. You may do something even smaller like try Bubble tea instead of your usual or the new Cambodian restaurant instead. Join a Meetup and get yourself on a mailing list or WhatsApp group if you want to meet others and have a break from life that will boost your batteries at the same time.

---

[37] *Sheldon, K. M., Boehm, J. K., & Lyubomirsky, S. (2012). Variety is the spice of happiness: The hedonic adaptation prevention (HAP) model. In I. Boniwell & S. David (Eds.), Oxford handbook of happiness (pp. 901–914). Oxford, UK: Oxford University Press.*

Think about what you could do that's different and a little unusual by making a list of random things you've always wanted to try and pick one to do this week. You can do these with a friend or family, but pick one, commit, and do it. Add some spice to that life!

Variety list:

Strategy 22: Talk to yourself, but do it right!

Self-talk

We can remain interested and engaged with our activities through self-talk[38]. But, we tend not to use it well, or judge its quality and that's a problem because what we say to ourselves has the same impact as others saying it to us. So, if we call ourselves dumb for example, our emotions merely follow and our actions aren't far behind. Yet, there are times we might enjoy a perfectly good activity, but listen to our self-talk too much and talk ourselves out of doing it. How many of you skipped the gym because you told yourself you were feeling under the weather but ended up cleaning the house anyways?

Our self-talk can help us stay on track or unfortunately, fall off track too. Thus, the trick with self-talk is knowing when to listen and when not to, as well as how to change it when it is no longer useful.

How is your self-talk? Think of a situation you are facing and consider how your self-talk helps. Does it bring out the best of you or create insecurity or doubt? Create new self-talk that is more realistic, positive, or functional. You can practice with different types of self-talk that suit many situations, optimize your excellence, and increase positive emotion. Try the new self-talk this week and record how it went.

Yet, don't pretend all is perfect, we make mistakes and we're not always at our best. In these cases, aim for realistic self-talk where you accept your mistakes and move forward without judgement.

---

[38] *Hardy, J., Hall, C. R., & Alexander, M. R. (2001). Exploring self-talk and affective states in sport. Journal of Sports Sciences, 19, 469-475; Gammage, K. L., Hardy, J., & Hall, C.R. (2001). A description of self-talk in exercise. Psychology of Sport and Exercise, 2, 233-247.*

Rehashing mistakes won't change anything. Notice the mistake, make amends, solve it and move on. The self-talk should end there.
My current self-talk is….

The result of this self-talk is… (what it makes me do)?

My better self-talk would sound like....

The results of my new self-talk would be...

Strategy 23: It's okay to fail.

Self-compassion

We're tough on ourselves, especially when things aren't going well. We feel we've failed, don't measure up, or aren't enough and these views can lead us to dropping out of activities that can help us grow and become better versions of ourselves. But, know that these messages are shaped by negative emotions. When we feel happier, we tend to think better of ourselves, but when we feel negatively, negative thoughts follow. But, until these emotions change, what can you do in the meanwhile?

Use self-compassion[39], the same compassion you'd use for your friends, siblings, mother, or son. It's not about feeling sorry for yourself, it's accepting that you feel bad and giving yourself permission to feel that way while offering yourself the same encouragement and kindness you'd give others. You can do this by writing yourself a letter like this one.

"Dear me,

You're stressed; you have deadlines and work is relentless. You have meetings tomorrow and you're not ready. You feel like life is pushing you like a bottle on the ocean. But, remember that it gets this way every so often, and every time, you make it through. This is no different. Stop what you're doing for 10 minutes and listen. You're going to go for a walk around the house or wherever you are. Put a few things away, wash your hands, stretch your legs, and drink some water. Listen to one song. Just one. And if you feel like you need to cry, then do. But you only have 10 minutes to refocus. Set the timer on your phone and go. At the end of 10 minutes, come back and finish reading this letter...

---

[39] *Neff, K. (2003). Self-compassion: An alternative conceptualization of a healthy attitude toward oneself. Self and Identity, 2(2), 85–101.*

You are amazing and you're going to do great things sooner than you think, so hang on and do your best. And if you fall, you fall. You'll just get up and do it again. People have fallen from higher. They've survived, you will too. So, work a bit more for today, get some sleep and face tomorrow like the magnificent person you are. I believe in you."

Write yourself a letter for when things go bad. You know what advice you need to hear. You can keep it in your bag, wallet or desk, so when it's a bad day, the letter is ready and you'll feel better fast.

If this is tough; think of a friend or family member who needs support and write them a letter instead. It's often easier to see the positives in other's lives. When you're finished with theirs, write yours. Keep that in mind when you're feeling down; encouraging others to see the positive helps us do the same.

Dear me...

Strategy 24: It's the opposite of depression

Flow

Flow[40] is the emotional reward we get from achieving a sense of competence and excellence over time in things like sports, music, the arts, or even doing surgery, academic research or other concentrated work. Anything can bring on flow as long as it is difficult, uses skills and talent, and requires an investment of time. In flow, we:

- Take control; we are doing, partaking, and responding. We are not just watching life or events go by.
- Concentrate and think of nothing but the activity. We are narrowly focused and lose track of time.
- Do not worry about our self-image, i.e., hair, or clothes, and let competitors worry about themselves.
- Select difficult tasks and use skills in ways we've not done before or more than usual causing us to grow.
- Respond to feedback that tells us what to do next by interpreting and 'reading' the activity and ourselves.
- Consider the activity gratifying and are excited for it. Flow is rare in activities we are forced to do.

Flow only emerges when we develop ability and don't have to think much. We are self-conscious when we take on new activity, we're learning; but in time, we forget about ourselves and focus on doing and being. This brings on flow, where we detach from the world and focus on our experience in the absence of thought. It is the opposite of depression as it forces the mind to be positively occupied.

---

[40] *Csikszentmihalyi, M. (1990). Flow: The psychology of optimal experience. New York, NY: Harper & Row.*

Have you experienced a state of flow before? How often do you experience it these days? How many times a day, week, or month? Doing what?

Some people don't experience flow. They may be too self-conscious about taking part in activity. Others avoid hard work and prefer an easy life. Others participate but give up too soon, while others have not found the right fit and change activity too often. Some feel that being an adult precludes the participation in what appears to be "play," while many don't see the point of doing anything at all! Yet, participation is vital as the usual life challenges we face versus those we create and direct do not offer us the means to develop our skills. We also don't learn from them in the same way we learn from weekly tennis matches for example, which rely on discipline, focus, confidence, strength, and mastery over our emotions and actions. If you don't experience flow, why do you think this is the case?

How can you change your mind about the way in which you engage with life's activities so that you can experience more flow?

Getting flow...

Here are a few questions people have asked about flow.

- What activity will bring on flow?

Anything that involves effort, time, skills, and challenge like doing weights, sculpture, playing the violin, writing a novel, or flying a plane! None are easy, but all possible in time with focus and effort.

- What if I'm not good at anything?

Everyone has talents; you just don't know yours yet. Give yourself permission to try new activities. Don't look for something you're good at, look for something you like and can be good at.

- I've tried something and I'm really not good at it.

That's what practice is for. Growth doesn't come from doing something a few times, so give it a good chance. But, sometimes you just don't like it. Try something else.

- I like what I'm doing, but can't focus. My thoughts wander.

If you have the mental space to think of the past or present, your activity is too easy. Increase its difficulty, complexity or intensity to force your focus. Stop thinking; do.

In what activity could you generate flow? Is it new or something you are already doing?

How will you deal with adaptation given that it interferes with the experience of flow?

How will you deal with overthinking which also interferes with the experience of flow?

Is there is anything else that stops you from being absorbed in learning and perfecting something tough? What can you do about it?

Strategy 25: Sitting disease.

Physical activity

We've been talking about behavior and thoughts, but movement gets forgotten in the quest for happiness despite its role in reducing depression and boosting positive emotions and self-efficacy, self-control, and confidence. The role of physical movement in positivity is more vital than you'd expect and unfortunately, we don't move much these days. Whether at work, university, or home, we spend a lot of time sitting. It's not only the working hours, it's our recreational and commuting hours that are spent sitting too. Chatting with friends, driving, going out for dinner; the truth is we sit more than any other activity.

This has consequences for health and happiness; the less you move, the less oxygen you get and the slower your heart rate, which affects your thoughts, mood and energy[41]. Physical activity, especially aerobic exercise boosts the brain's ability to regenerate brain cells and levels of serotonin, both of which play a role in preventing and treating depression[42]. Physical activity also regulates sleep, which in itself increases positive mood. Luckily, your body responds to short bursts of movement, so every 40 minutes or so, get up, walk around for a few minutes and swing your arms. If you can't do that in the office, or other public space, go to the bathroom and do it in private.

---

[41] Dunstan, D., Barr, E., Healy, G., Salmon, J., Shaw, J., Balkau, B., ..., & Owen, N. (2010). Television viewing time and mortality: The Australian diabetes, obesity and lifestyle study (AusDiab). Circulation, 121(3), 384-391.

[42] Szuhany, K. L., Bugatti, M., & Otto, M. W. (2014). A meta-analytic review of the effects of exercise on brain-derived neurotrophic factor. Journal of Psychiatric Research, 60C, 56–64.

Do you move enough? Calculate the time you spend sitting and sleeping to understand the importance of sitting disease. Add up all the minutes you spend sitting in a day whether it's working, reading, watching television, driving, etc. How many minutes is it?

What can you do to move more in the day? Small things count like parking further away from entrances, getting off transportation one stop early and walking the rest of the way. You can even send fewer emails and walk to someone's desk or house instead. Note 5 things.

Now, choose 1 and do it as often as you can.

Strategy 26: Everyone needs it.

Sleep, food and water

When babies cry, it's easy to know what the problem is; they are hungry, thirsty, or tired. We understand the relationship between mood and food. Yet, we're poor at recognizing the same in ourselves. We have equal requirements and depend on food, water, sleep and activity for the fuel to get through the day with the ability to control our emotions and regulate motivation. You would never dream of delaying a child's lunch by three hours, that's only asking for an emotional breakdown of massive proportions; why do it to yourself?

It's not only about delaying or skipping meals, it's about skimping on sleep too. A lack of sleep impacts energy, concentration, interest, and most of all, the ability to create a positive mindset[43]. Maybe it's temporary and you can't sleep because you're worrying about problems, or you can sleep but ignore your body's needs and update Instagram, watch movies, or eat instead. Maybe you sleep the right amount of time but at odd hours thinking a nap will make up for it.

You know yourself best. What do you need to do in this area?

How about going to sleep and waking up at the same time, even on weekends? Describe what you do now; what could you do instead.

---

[43] *Hamilton, N. A., Nelson, C. A., Stevens, N., & Kitzman, H. (2007). Sleep and psychological well-being. Social Indicators Research, 82(1), 147-163.*

How about packing your lunch and a snack for work or school? Describe what you do now and what you could do instead.

How about drinking some water every hour and moving? Describe what you do now and what you could do instead.

Introduce one change this week and do it repeatedly. Once it's become part of your lifestyle, start with the next change.

Strategy 27: Too much, too soon.

Rising aspirations

There are other things that interfere with our ability to stick with activity and experience flow and that is jumping ahead too soon, or having rising aspirations[44]. As we reach goals and attain better circumstances, we naturally and quickly develop greater dreams. While this is normal and keeps us wanting and getting more, it can also result in the inability to enjoy what we have. In effect, we look ahead too soon.

Let's take Shamsa. She joined the Sharrif Corporation three years ago and had big ambitions to move ahead in the company. She is good at her job and often recognized. She got her first promotion after eight months and quickly went from being an assistant to a junior and now, a middle level executive. She has her sights on upper management and is working hard to get there. Yet, listen to what she said to her friend this week. "Amna, I feel like I haven't accomplished anything. I feel I should be further ahead, like I'm not there yet…"

Amna was left speechless as they both started with the company at the same time and Amna is still in the same role. "What do you mean you've accomplished nothing? Are you kidding?! You've been promoted the most and the most quickly? Everyone is envious of you all the time! And anyways, where is this "there" you feel you should be? Honestly, you wouldn't be happy if you were made CEO!"

Amna may have been harsh, but she's not wrong. Shamsa's rising aspirations are to blame; the moment she reaches a goal, she moves

---

[44] *Chancellor, J., & Lyubomirsky, S. (2011). Happiness and thrift: When (spending) less is (hedonically) more. Journal of Consumer Psychology, 21, 131-138; Jacobs Bao, K., Layous, K., & Lyubomirsky, S. (2015). Aspirations and well-being: When are high aspirations harmful? Manuscript under review.*

to the next and never enjoys what she has accomplished. The more she gets, the more she wants, and the less happy she is.

To conquer rising aspirations, she needs to appreciate her positive changes well after they occur and find ways to enjoy and engage with the changes so as not to focus too quickly on future goals that can reduce her present happiness. She can set her sights on more, but she needs to enjoy the ride too; otherwise, what's the point of reaching aspirations if they bring no joy along the way?

Do you jump ahead too soon and not make time to enjoy your circumstances or the goals you've reached?

How can you slow your aspirations to get more joy out of what you've accomplished?

How have you resolved the balancing act of appreciating today, but focusing on more for tomorrow?

Strategy 28: Plan it, but don't do it!

Anticipation

Maitha and George are newly wedded and off to France. Both have been looking forward to Paris, the city of love, for years. To prepare for the trip, they read reviews of the best hotels by the Seine, the latest art galleries and quaint little bistros in which to eat. Maitha added a few interior design stores to visit and George found a few neighborhoods to walk in. They've been planning for months and the anticipation is high! Three weeks before their flight, they create a special calendar and mark off the days. Just the thought of being in Paris makes them smile and feel closer to one another.

It's the big day...They are late getting to the airport due to a flat tire. In the plane, they hit turbulence and George feels ill. When things settle, a baby starts to cry and continues for the rest of the flight. When they arrive in Paris, the passport official shouts instructions in French, which neither understand. Their luggage is lost and there is a transportation strike that started only hours before. Like it couldn't get worse, next to the hotel, which is nice, construction keeps them awake. It rains for 5 of the 7 days and George's office calls non-stop. It's not the trip they dreamt of, nor is it producing much happiness.

In fact, they are less happy on the actual trip than they were at home thinking of it. This is the problem with reality. It never lives up to expectation. Yet, the problem isn't the crying baby or missing luggage. It's that these were not in the picture they imagined, which acted as the standard against which they judged the event. If the real event was better than the imagined one, they would have been happy, but here, the real one was worse and created unhappiness. Had they just said, "let's hang out in Paris", it would have been easier to laugh about.

Think about your planned positive experiences; what is most pleasurable, the time before it, or the actual event? How something is experienced in reality can fall short of how it is imagined. In fact, having positive experiences can be less enjoyable than just thinking about them[45]. So, anticipate as much as you can ahead of time to generate as much positive emotion as possible. Dream about the scenes, possibilities, and best-case scenarios; then, stop dreaming before the event, drop all expectations and be open to what happens after that. See the anticipation as one event and the actual trip as another where you create a new experience based on what is in front of you and not what was in your head.

What's your strategy for dealing with anticipation?

---

[45] Richins, M. L. (2013). When wanting is better than having: Materialism, transformation expectations, and product-evoked emotions in the purchase process. Journal of Consumer Research, 40(1), 1-18.

Relationships

Our relationships with others can certainly bring great happiness. That's why all relationships count and not only intimate ones, but the connections we have with family, friends, and even strangers. Here are several strategies to help improve your relationships and create new ones too.

First, to which social networks and groups do you belong? No matter how strong (i.e., family, friends) or weak (i.e., neighbors, colleagues, social groups) these ties are, name them as they all matter.

They help us see in the dark

Relationships provide occasions for friendly competition, the practice of unfamiliar or well-used qualities, and the generation of new ideas. The more ties we have, the fuller our personalities also become as we use different sides of ourselves to deal with varied people. Relationships also help define who we are. You may be a daughter, brother, partner, parent, and friend, but without relationships, it's hard to know who we are. Connections provide us with roles and identities.

Without people, we lose touch with the boundaries of reality. Imagine you only had yourself to talk to, how would you know if you were inappropriate or exaggerating? The feedback we get from others is critical in coping with the world and disconnecting from others makes our thoughts unravel easily. People provide the limits of reality and we need to be told where those are sometimes.

How do you feel about your connections? Do you connect too much and not have time for yourself or not enough and end up talking to yourself all day? What would a good balance look like?

Strategy 29: Name it to improve it!

Find 3 good things

People have their quirks and while small, these can get in the way of strengthening relationships. This activity can help you interpret those oddities otherwise. Naming three good things in relationships[46] is a way to find and focus on the positives. Use this with relationships that are strained and reflect on the positive characteristics of that person. Or, you can positively reframe behaviors that bother you like the examples below. In the last column, think of a way that you can share what you see the other person doing so that they can be encouraged to do it more often.

Who?	Good thing	Good thing	Good thing	How will I share it?
Partner	He always tries to help (even if it's not helpful!)	He's thoughtful in his way, he opens doors for me.	He takes pride in his family, takes interest in our lives.	During our walk, I'll stop and say it.
Teenage daughter	She speaks her mind; she'll stand up for herself later.	She's an original and doesn't follow the crowd.	She is protective of her sister; family means something.	I'll write a note and leave it in her lunch box.

---

[46] *Jacobs Bao, K., & Lyubomirsky, S. (2013). Making it last: Combating hedonic adaptation in romantic relationships. Journal of Positive Psychology, 8, 196–206.*

Three good things

Who?	Good thing	Good thing	Good thing	How will I share this?

Strategy 30: Where to?

Make a Date

We can improve relationships by investing time in them[47], but having the same conversations over and over again won't make you closer; in fact, you'll soon adapt and be bored. So, plan a date! A date can be a coffee, walking, movie, or museum date; it can even be a gym date with a friend, colleague, or nephew. Move the conversation away from the usual and ask things like: what's your biggest joy in life? If you weren't afraid, what would you do? The conversation will go to new heights. To help, search online for "conversation starters." Plan three outings this month and call those people right now to reserve their time.

Outing 1. Who will I ask on a date? What will we do? When, where? How can I make it memorable?

---

[47] *Jacobs Bao, K., & Lyubomirsky, S. (2013). Making it last: Combating hedonic adaptation in romantic relationships. Journal of Positive Psychology, 8, 196–206.*

Outing 2. Who will I ask on a date? What will we do? When, where? How can I make it memorable?

Outing 3. Who will I ask on a date? What will we do? When, where? How can I make it memorable?

Strategy 31: Supersize that!

Social initiative

Are there people you've only met once at a conference, wedding, through other friends or at a neighbor's house? Why don't you be brave and organize a breakfast of interesting people you hardly know and ask them each to bring a friend? Don't pack the place full of your friends, but go mostly alone[48] so that you too are forced to meet new people. You can even set conversation cards on each plate and put a limit on how long each person sits in one place; one chair for starters, another for desert, a third for tea. With a broad mix, you'll surely find someone with which to connect and you'll be the breakfast queen everyone wants to meet.

Where:

When:

Who:

---

[48] *Coan, J. A., Schaefer, H. S., & Davison, R. J. (2006). Lending a hand: Social regulation of the neural response to threat. Psychological Science, 17, 1032–1039.*

Write the invite here and then text, email, IM, Tweet, etc., but send it!

Strategy 32: Mirror them.

Capitalization

Capitalization[49] refers to how we respond to others' good news and it's a way to increase our happiness and that of others too. But, capitalization also depends on how you share good news too.

What happens when you share good news? Do you get a good response? Are others excited and happy for you? How do you share it? Are you enthusiastic or do you minimize news, or not tell it at all?

[49] Gable, S. L., & Reis, H. T. (2010). Good news! Capitalizing on positive events in an interpersonal context. In M. P. Zanna (Ed.), Advances in Experimental Social Psychology (vol. 42, pp. 195-257). San Diego, CA: Elsevier Academic Press.

Let's look at Melanie, who landed an awesome project with the ministry. She worked on the proposal for months and it's her life's passion. She'll make good money, but it's more about the interesting research she'll do and that her career will grow. It also means others recognize her work. Melanie feels great and shares the news.

"Guess what, Anne? I got that project I've been working on--" "Wow!," responds Anne, "tell me all about it!"

Anne asks Melanie what she is looking forward to the most and what it means to her. She is curious, extends the conversation with questions to show interest and verbally shares her joy. She even copies Melanie's facial expression in empathy. Anne is using *active constructive* responding. It's not just listening; it's taking part in the story and constructing positive emotions between herself and Melanie by being curious and showing care. Being happy for other people is one thing, but extending their news and helping them capitalize on their own emotion takes relationships to a higher level.

Melanie tries to share with Mark. "Remember I told you about the project I've been working on? I got the news; I won the contract!"

"Oh, good. Hey, did you see Jalal? I need to ask him something."

Melanie's positive emotions immediately fade given Mark's polite, yet indifferent response. She lost her positivity, but Mark also lost the chance to capitalize on Melanie's emotions for himself. Capitalization is not only for the person sharing the news; it's also for the person hearing it like Anne who also felt positively as a result of absorbing Melanie's emotions. Capitalization extends everyone's positivity and that's why we should be more mindful of how we share good news as well as respond to that of others.

Am I happy for others? If not, why? What do you think might happen if you were to share in the joy of others? (If this doesn't apply to you, why do you think others don't want to show their joy in response to others good news? Does what they fear actually happen?)

How can I change my responses (facial expressions, actions, verbal responses) to other's good news so that I can get more positive results for myself and deepen my relationships with them too?

Are there certain people for whom I can be happy and not others? What might be so bad about being happy for someone you like less than others?

Strategy 33: Give to get.

Kind acts I

Ten. That's all you need. Kind acts, that is.

Extending kindness[50] to others is one of the simplest ways we can boost our happiness and while 10 acts might sound like a lot, it's easier than you think. But first, what do kind acts do for you?

For one, they get you outside of your head. We spend an awful lot of time up there and that can be time spent stewing, obsessing, or analyzing. When we're focused on doing kind acts, we necessarily have to focus on others and outside of ourselves.

Further, when you're focused on doing a kind act for others, your positive emotions already get a boost. Anticipating what you'll do and what their reaction will be gets us feeling more positively even before we've done it. It also makes us more playful, especially when we remain open to seeing how we can be kind to strangers and that openness, whether we act on it or not, can free our minds from focusing on ourselves. And while we don't do acts of kindness for the purpose of getting anything in return, that possibility always exists.

Finally, performing kind acts allows us to feel like better people, use our strengths and develop relationships[51]. Doing good makes us feel good and over time, makes us good. It's a win-win for everyone.

Can you give 10 compliments today? Yep, 10.

---

[50] *Otake, K., Shimai, S., Tanaka-Matsumi, J., Otsui, K., & Fredrickson, B. L. (2006). Happy people become happier through kindness: A counting kindnesses intervention. Journal of Happiness Studies, 7(3), 361–375.*

[51] *Aknin, L. B., & Dunn, E. W. (2013). Spending money on others leads to higher happiness than spending on yourself. In J. F. Froh & A. C. Parks (Eds.), Activities for teaching positive psychology: A guide for instructors (pp. 93-98). Washington, DC: APA.*

You can come back here and note how these made you feel and what positive responses you received in return. Keep in mind not all of the compliments you give will be acknowledged or even appreciated. That's okay. You be you and let them worry about themselves.

How did the compliment giving go?

This week, complete as many good deeds as possible. You may think this feels fake and you're only doing it to fill the page, but your motivation for doing this does not matter right now. The point is to do them and develop a giving style that reflects your way of doing things. After, note three highlights and insights you had. Remember, some good deeds will backfire and for reasons you may never know. Don't worry about it.

Good deed #1:

How did I feel after doing this?

Good deed #2:

How did I feel after doing this?

Good deed #3:

How did I feel after doing this?

Strategy 34: More good deeds...

Kind acts II

If you liked the good deed activity, keep it up by creating a good deed club with family or neighbors. You can even combine these with a weekly breakfast among friends (i.e., good deeds for an hour on Al Hambra Street and then breakfast for all!). You can even do a good deed marathon for a 24-hour period once a month with a group of like-minded individuals, or go all out and organize 11 friends (plus you) to meet once a month and donate an amount of money into a pool with the winner choosing the charity to which it will go that month. There are many ways to give; ask people around you for their ideas and go from there.

Develop ideas that you think could be fun and then send an invitation to complete one with friends and family in the next week or two.

Ideas for a good deed club:

Strategy 35: The magic word.

Gratitude

There is another way to improve relationships and it's by saying "Thanks." Because gratitude promotes the savoring of positive experiences and reduces anger and depression[52], it's a good strategy.

Select a person who has had a positive influence in your life and write them a letter of gratitude. Let them know what they did and how it made you feel. Handwrite it so that the person has a lasting memory of your thoughts. Once written, meet them in person and read it, or call them and read it. At a minimum, mail it. If the person has passed on, read it to them as though they were there.

This is an activity you can do repeatedly. You can choose one day of the week and write a letter to a different person, or do a gratitude day and write as many letters as you can. What's fun is the boost you get writing the letter and the one that comes when they respond.

What if you get an unexpected response? Like all strategies, the odd one may backfire, so decide whether you need to take action. Is their response typical? Do they have current issues happening? Are there things that happened in the meanwhile that caused offense? If so, use this as an opportunity to repair relationships. Not everyone will respond positively or at all. That does not diminish your sentiment. See these letters as an opening to better relationships and not an end in themselves.

---

[52] DeWall, C. N., Lambert, N. M., Pond, R. S., Jr., Kashdan, T. B., & Fincham, F. D. (2012). A grateful heart is a non-violent heart: Cross-sectional, experience sampling, longitudinal, and experimental evidence. *Social Psychological and Personality Science, 3,* 232-240. Duckworth, A. L., Steen, T. A., Seligman, M. E. P. (2005). Positive psychology in clinical practice. *Annual Review of Clinical Psychology, 1,* 629-651.

Make a list of the people to whom you want to write letters here.

Dear…

Strategy 36: Build your circle.

Network

While we live in an age of hyper-connectedness, it's also strangely the era of loneliness. Increasingly, people report feeling lonely or unpopular when they might in fact have friends, just not 917 of them like Facebook would have you believe is normal! Sometimes, it really is the case that there's few people in our lives due to life transitions like illness, having children, graduating from university or moving. Whatever the situation, unless you're super social, most of us could stand to socialize a bit more and we can do that by changing our minds about what connections mean[53] and what they are for.

Creating a social circle from nothing takes work and is scary, but it doesn't need to be. Instead of thinking "I have few friends", consider, "I'm open for business and have space for more!" Change your approach and look for other individuals who also seem open for business (and perhaps going through the same transitions) and extend an invitation for coffee, dinner, or a movie by casually saying, 'I'm about to have lunch, would you like to join me?' as an example.

The other way is to think of yourself as a connector versus someone who needs friends. You can do this by inviting colleagues or classmates who look interesting and ask them to bring one other person for coffee, dinner, bowling, or a walk; whatever suits you.

The aim is to build a professional and social network that will be useful in time. Plus, it's a way to get to know people, find out what their goals are, and see how you could help one another. The smart ones will recognize the opportunity and those are the ones you want! Repeat once a month by adding new people each time. It'll become easier to do and everyone will want to join; that's how you build a social circle, one person at a time.

---

[53] *Mogilner, C. (2010). The pursuit of happiness: Time, money, and social connection. Psychological Science, 21(9), 1348–1354.*

Choose your people now and send an invitation. Don't worry if the first time flops either, you'll know how to do it differently the next.

Strategy 37: Where are they?

Reconnect

You're working now and perhaps some of your school or university friends went elsewhere and you've lost touch. Think not only of high school but even junior school, and primary school; did you have a best friend that you lost touch with? When was the last time you spoke? Do you know what's become of them?

Why don't you make it your mission to track them down and reconnect? You might need to go through other friends, teachers, your parent's friends, or even search online. Once you've found them, give them a call, Skype or text them, write them a letter or pay them a visit and ask whether they remember the time when you....? Reminiscing positively about the past can be beneficial and help us see how much we've grown, changed, and accomplished[54].

For now, write down their name and if you know how to get in touch, send a text now so you don't forget. If you don't know where they are, search on Facebook, Google, or wherever else you think you could find them. If you can, connect with them in the coming week.

With whom will you connect?

---

[54] *Westerhof, G., Bohlmeijer, E., & Webster, J. (2010). Reminiscence and mental health: A review of recent progress in theory, research and interventions. Ageing and Society, 30(4), 697–721.*

Strategy 38: Let go.

Forgiveness

Have you been betrayed or hurt by a friend or family member? Devastating events like these put a massive strain on relationships and inflict a lot of stress in terms of deciding what to do about them. On the one hand, you may be justified in feeling angry. On the other, it takes so much effort to stay mad. When someone wrongs us, it seems to hurt less if we stay angry. But, consider the cost of doing so. The energy you spend directed at that person takes a toll. It's something you always think of and it removes attention from things that would bring you joy. It drains you physically and keeps you up at night. Remembering what they did makes you relive the event and stresses your body.

What do you think of forgiveness[55]?

Before you say no, hold on. Staying angry, upset, or worked up means that you continue to give that person power and control over your feelings and thoughts and that keeps you a prisoner, not them. Forgiveness is not always about others; it's about making a choice to not hurt yourself any more.

---

[55] *McCullough, M. E., Root, L. M., & Cohen A. D. (2006). Writing about the benefits of an interpersonal transgression facilitates forgiveness. Journal of Consulting and Clinical Psychology, 74, 887–897.*

Can you write a letter? It'll have 4 parts to it and will take time. You can do it in stages; there is no rush. It's a letter to yourself anyways.

a.	Can you write a letter – to yourself – trying to understand why they did what they did and what they were feeling that made them do it? Use your most mature, peaceful, wise and understanding self to do this and remember that you are not speaking to them, you're trying to understand it like an outside observer.

b.	Can you consider whether there was something in your behavior that might have led to it? There may not have been anything but it's worth taking a look. Think carefully. Sometimes you may not think there was anything, but if you put yourself in the other person's shoes, thinking like they do, it is possible.

c.	Talk about what it has cost you to hold on to the anger, hurt, and/or betrayal. How has holding on to the incident and reviewing it repeatedly hurt you over time?

d.	Finally, find three good things that came from the situation. You might not think there are any, but you might be wiser, more selective, and more purposeful about life. Think broadly.

My letter…

Strategy 39: Play nicely.

Connect with others

Are the streets in your city or town as friendly as they could be? The next time you're in public, notice how strangers respond to you. In most places around the world, they're probably trying to avoid making eye contact and escape being seen. An unwritten rule says look around, above, or through, but never at others. And if we do, it's for a purpose; to give an answer or directions.

What if we started to look at people – not in a prolonged stare – but merely long enough to acknowledge they exist with a nod of the head and a slight smile of friendliness? Wouldn't it be nice to live in a world where a nod of the head meant, "Hello fellow human, I see you and I wish you well today?" This activity may feel strange, so only do what makes you comfortable; yet, recognizing the existence of others only takes a second and that's all it takes to create greater tolerance and better ties and connections[56] in society.

What would it be like for you to smile or nod your head at three random people today? Go ahead; try it. What response did you get?

---

[56] *Vacharkulksemsuk, T., & Fredrickson, B. L. (2012). Strangers in sync: Achieving embodied rapport through shared movements. Journal of Experimental Social Psychology, 48, 399-402.*

Was it strange for you?

What difference would it make to your day to remain open to others instead of closed unto yourself?

Strategy 40: Have a horrid dinner party.

Connections

Here you go. You have permission to host the worst dinner party if it means being able to have fun and see your friends more often. We worry about being a perfect host, cooking the perfect dish, serving the best wine and as a result, avoid creating excellent social situations for ourselves where we could increase our positive emotions and deepen relationships. Yet, if you remember the best parties you've ever attended, they were likely the ones where you laughed the most versus those with the fanciest napkin rings.

Forget perfection, mix it up[57]. Here's how to host a terrible party:

- Tell everyone not to dress up; whatever they have on is okay.

- Give everyone the alert that if you cook, it'll be what it'll be, or expect take-out. No major grocery shopping allowed.

- Ask everyone to pitch in for beverages.

- Clear a space where it'll happen and nowhere else. A living room table and chairs will do. Clean the bathroom. Close the doors to the other rooms. Easy. (You can also turn this into a picnic and go to a park, or have it in your yard).

- Ask your best DJ friend to take care of the music.

- Have games on hand, or conversation starter cards for help.

Voila. A party where you can relax, enjoy your friends and laugh all night. Martha Stewart or Nigella Lawson would not be amused and well, that's reason to be happy right there, no!? (wink)

---

[57] *Sheldon, K. M., Boehm, J. K., & Lyubomirsky, S. (2012). Variety is the spice of happiness: The hedonic adaptation prevention (HAP) model. In I. Boniwell & S. David (Eds.), Oxford handbook of happiness (pp. 901–914). Oxford, UK: Oxford University Press.*

Who do you want at your dinner party?

When? Where and what? (Keep it simple, dear; fun is the goal).

Meaning and Purpose

There are even more ways to be happy in life; some are focused on immediate positive emotions, while others are focused on deeper values and life purpose. In this section, we explore the value of meaning and consider how it might apply to you.

Meaning involves participating in something bigger than us, like volunteering for a charity. It can also involve our personal values or religious beliefs. In short, meaning[58] is what connects ideas, objects, and people to one another; it is the why of what we do and the purpose we give ourselves for taking action. When individuals give a reason or understand why they organize their lives in such a way, purpose emerges[59]. But, don't feel like you must have it all figured out, it's enough to have a purpose *right now* and it can be something like training for a marathon or caring for your children.

Meaning changes over time in the face of life events like accidents, illness, or bombings. As we are natural meaning makers, we automatically ask "why" and this helps us cope and make sense of life. On the other hand, we also need to know when to stop asking why. Sometimes things just happen and other times, things do happen for a reason, but it's just not your reason; you might merely be an actor in someone else's story. Meaning can even emerge at the oddest times, so we need to stay open to opportunities like talking to a stranger on a bus who can offer a new perspective on life.

---

[58] *Heine, S. J., Proulx, T., & Vohs, K. D. (2006). The meaning maintenance model: On the coherence of social motivations. Personality and Social Psychology Review, 10, 88-110.*
[59] *Steger, M. F. (2012). Making meaning in life. Psychological Inquiry, 23, 381–385.*

Strategy 41: What's important?

Values

Affirming values[60] or redefining purpose involves reminding yourself of who you are, what you stand for, and who is in your life to help you live according to those values and get the life you want. Thinking about the bigger picture can help reorient our thoughts and actions in line with our beliefs and is useful when we're feeling lost. Reorienting ourselves to values can even reduce physical stress.

What are your values? What's important to you? Examples might be hard work, integrity, benevolence, etc. Choose three of your highest values and explain how these show up in your daily life.

Value 1.

---

[60] *Creswell, J. D., Welch, W. T., Taylor, S.E., Taylor, S. E., & Mann, T. (2005). Affirmation of personal values buffers neuroendocrine and psychological stress responses. Society, 16, 846–852.*

Value 2.

Value 3.

Who helps you live your best life in accordance with your values?

Is there a situation you're facing that could benefit from you taking actions that are more in line with who you really are, rather than the person others want you to be? If you acted on your values, what difference would it make to the situation and how you feel about yourself? Explain and find a solution for your dilemma.

Strategy 42: It needs to match.

Time use

Although we value things like health or learning, we can tell whether these things really matter by looking at our use of time[61]. Does your use of time reflect what matters to you? This is not always possible given time constraints or other limitations but the closer we live to our values, the better we feel. A match between the two is important.

Consider how you spent time this week. Note where, with whom, and what you were doing to see whether it matches. If not, what changes can you make to live more closely to what you say matters?

Day/Time	Morning	At work	After work	Evening
Sunday				

[61] Diener, E., Ng, W., & Tov, W. (2009). Balance in life and declining marginal utility of diverse resources. Applied Research in Quality of Life, 3, 277–291.

Monday				
Tuesday				
Wednesday				

Thursday				
Friday				
Saturday				

How do you feel about how you spend your time? Are there things that don't match and bring no meaning or sense of purpose? Are there things you'd like to change? Discuss your thoughts and any changes you'd like to implement.

Strategy 43: Turn it off.

Disconnect from social media

Could you disconnect from social media for 48 hours?

While social media can be really great in connecting with people from long ago, across the city, or far away, it can also just as easily get in the way of meaningful conversations, growth-inducing experiences, sleep, physical activity, and actual enjoyment! Social media can even limit our ability to soak up positive emotions. Plus, social media even has the potential to make us unhappy[62] as it's impossible not to compare ourselves with perfect Instagram accounts and Facebook fairytales that no matter how much we know are staged, make us feel bad about our lives in comparison. In fact, a number of experts find that taking a social media fast can improve psychological outcomes and make us happier with ourselves, our lives, as well as the people in it and be more reflective about what's really important in life beyond that selfie!

Do you think you've got what it takes to do a social media cleanse?

No Facebook, Twitter, Instagram, WhatsApp for 48 hours. If you really need to connect, call like your grandparents did. If there's an emergency, someone will call you. You won't miss a thing; in fact, you'll have time you never knew you had to paint, sew, play with your niece, go for a run, visit a museum, or play a board game (remember those?). To help, send your contacts a message saying "On a social media retreat, will be in touch in 48 hours" so no one panics and sends the police! Then, disable the internet connection.

---

[62] *Chou, H. T. G., & Edge, N. (2012). "They are happier and having better lives than I am": The impact of using Facebook on perceptions of others' lives. Cyberpsychology, Behavior, and Social Networking, 15(2), 117-121.*

You can disconnect once a week if you find this productive or however much you choose; it's not a must to be connected after all.

How do I feel about taking this challenge? Nervous? Worried? Excited? Stressed? (oh dear!)

When shall I begin the challenge? Make it easy – a weekend is easiest.

What was it like? Will I do this again?

Strategy 44: How are you 'adulting'?

Getting perspective

It's startling, but as much as we are mature adults, many of us still wonder whether we're "adulting" acceptably? Having a full-time job or even kids is sometimes not enough to make us feel secure about our abilities in life. Yet, you've clearly made good choices in life so far[63], you wouldn't have gotten here otherwise.

Thinking of your decisions and where you've taken your life so far, of what are you most proud?

---

[63] *Peters, M. L., Flink, I. K., Boersma, K., & Linton, S. J. (2010). Manipulating optimism: Can imagining a best possible self be used to increase positive future expectancies? Journal of Positive Psychology, 5, 204–211.*

What were some of the best decisions you took in life? How did those positively influence your life?

What would be your best piece of advice for someone starting out their adult life and why?

Strategy 45: Do good.

Giving

Another way in which we can boost our happiness and meaning is to develop and pursue a project dedicated to the service of others[64]. Giving, whether it's time, money, or resources makes us feel good, but more than that, it makes us consider the plight of others and reinforces a sense of compassion and solidarity we have towards them. Yet, it's not only about feeling empathy for others, it's about actively doing something for them with the bonus that we feel a greater sense of control over our world.

Can you be the answer to one of the world's problems on a smaller scale? For example, if homelessness is a problem in your area and winter is approaching, why don't you organize a clothing drive at work or between all of your friends, family and neighbors? You could call it the "Bring 1 thing" project and encourage everyone to bring one thing, a shirt, a pair of socks, gloves, a book, and old pair of eye glasses or whatever is needed, and collect the goods over a specified period of time. You can even take to social media and put the call out to large numbers of people and really have an impact. You can come up with any idea actually; there is so much need and you can do a lot.

---

[64] Borgonovi, F. (2008). Doing well by doing good. The relationship between formal volunteering and self-reported health and happiness. Social Science and Medicine, 66, 2321–2334.

For now, note five ideas – you can decide on these later.

Which will I pick and who can I get to help me? How? Where? When?

Strategy 46: Begin with the end.

Appreciation

We are often told to take a long-term approach to life when it comes to health or education. For example, we know we need to exercise to live longer, study now to get a good career later, and choose a partner wisely so we can be happy now and in the future. This is true, but focusing exclusively on the future can also make us focus less on the present and away from maximizing our positivity on a daily basis. On the other hand, focusing too much on the present can make us blind to the reality that all good things come to an end. What we can do instead is contrast today with the 'end' – in essence, shortening time so every moment seems like the last of its kind[65].

The point is not to think of "the end" per se; but, rather, to be more appreciative and mindful of the present. For example, consider if today was your last day at work; what would you appreciate about it most? What would you do differently to make it meaningful? Could you share that appreciation now instead of waiting until the end? By shifting our view to the possible end and pretending that event, situation, or contact with someone may be the last, we appreciate it more and change how we approach what we do and say. It helps to remember that times passes quickly and needs to be cherished.

---

[65] Layous, K., Kurtz, J., Chancellor, J. & Lyubomirsky, S. (2017). Reframing the ordinary: Imagining time as scarce increases well-being. The Journal of Positive Psychology, doi: 10.1080/17439760.2017.1279210

Consider that today was your last day in this city before you moved away: what and who would you appreciate most? Is there anyone you'd like to thank? Would there be any last activity you'd like to do; have your favorite lunch in your favorite spot? If you thought it might be the last time you met with a friend, what would you want to say, ask, or even do? If you thought it was the last phone call to your parents, what would you want to say? Why don't you make every day a more meaningful one by thinking not only of the short-term, but of the 'last' of such events, and share the appreciation you have for those events, places and people?

Go ahead and do it.

Accomplishment

Accomplishments involve using our skills and efforts toward goals and this can be a source of happiness. Accomplishments are so important that we sometimes even pursue them in the absence of positive emotion, meaning, or relationships and do things for no other reason than to say, 'Yes, I did it!'

Friendly competition can be used to bring out the best in one another. When I engage in co-opetition with others, we effectively agree to push one another past our limits so that we can grow and experience personal excellence. Being clear on the goal of coopetition can help attain a sense of achievement even if failure is involved as competing is not actually designed for winning, but to pull the greatness out of us.

Think of what you've accomplished and what you have still to achieve in this next section.

Strategy 47: Reverse the bucket.

Past positives

You've heard of a "bucket list." It is a mental list on which we note things we'd like to do before it's too late. Items may include: travel to Kenya on safari; jump out of an airplane; open a business or write a novel before I'm 50. However, it's worth looking at our old lists too, things we've already done to see how far we've come and how blessed[66] we are in terms of opportunities we've had that others have not.

What have you done that stands out in memory? What have been your accomplishments to date (big and small)? Beside each item you've accomplished, write down what it was about you that helped to make that event successful.

For example:

Item 1: I learned to play the violin and played my first concert at the age of 23.

How did I make it happen? I was insanely dedicated and resisted all forms of instant gratification – even though it made me miserable at the time. When all of my friends were having fun, I was practicing. It really paid off in the end, who has a concert at the age of 23?! That remains a huge highlight of my life.

---

[66] *Emmons, R. A., & McCullough, M. E. (2003). Counting blessings versus burdens: An experimental investigation of gratitude and subjective well-being in daily life. Journal of Personality and Social Psychology, 84, 377–389.*

Item 2:

Item 3:

Item 4:

Item 5:

Strategy 48: The real bucket list

Goals and aspirations

You want to do a real bucket list, don't you?! It is inspiring and motivating to make a list and it is fun to dream and anticipate. Why not? You've got a long life ahead and many days to fill. Most of those will be consumed by work, sleep, and hopefully, having fun. Naturally, you will also have lows too and some of these will be completely out of your control. So, how about you control what you can and come up with that list?

What do you want to accomplish, do, and see[67]? Don't think about what you want to become – that'll come later; for now, think about the activities you'd want to fill your time with.

Here are a few examples from my life.

I really want to publish and sell this book – so, if you liked it, don't pass it on, tell your friends to buy it!

I'd like to go to a Viennese ball and wear a poufy dress and waltz to Vivaldi with a great man (tacky, lame, I know, but it's my list!)

I'd like to take a hot air balloon over the African plains.

You get where I'm going. Write it on the next page.

---

[67] *Mayser, S., Scheibe, S., & Riediger, M. (2008). (Un)reachable? An empirical differentiation of goals and life-longings. European Psychologist, 13, 126–140.*

Strategy 49: What about you?

Purpose

As you're thinking about your life, let's keep looking forward. You may have heard that to be satisfied in life, we need a purpose, a project, a reason for being, or a life goal that directs our energy. Yet, the search for purpose can be frightening and pressure people to have it all figured out. Honestly, most people can't articulate their purpose; so, you're not alone! But, why have a purpose anyways?

Purpose, something to do in life that reflects our values, personality, needs and desires and in which we spend a lot of time and want to do, can help us be motivated and set goals. It provides a sense of meaning in life too; when we have a purpose, our actions and decisions make sense, they don't just happen. Having purpose also reduces stress as we don't have to wonder what to do every day or why. We see a role for ourselves and a reason for it. Purpose increases our satisfaction with life too[68].

You're thinking...that sounds great, but how do you get purpose?

---

[68] *Park, N., Park, M., & Peterson, C. (2010). When is the search for meaning related to life satisfaction? Applied Psychology: Health and Well-Being, 2(1), 1-13.*

What makes you come alive? What issues do you care about in the world? What needs improving? List what you are passionate about.

Now, think of your skills and strengths that can help these issues. Is there a smaller role for you to play in your community, at work, university, or in your family now? How can you make a difference?

You can also think of the things for which you are grateful, i.e., support, guidance, knowledge, etc. Can you give these to others?

To help, interview people you find interesting and who have led a successful, positive life. They could be entrepreneurs making cupcakes, athletes, directors, bloggers, artists, a parent, or chef. They don't need to be famous. Find out how they got started; what strengths did they use? What advice do they have? How did they know what they wanted to do? Speak with them to get ideas. If nothing else, you pass time listening to someone interesting.

Strategy 50: Why not now?

Planning for success

This next activity might not apply to all of you, but read through and try it anyways. You never know until someone asks you whether you might have some ingenious idea to change the world. It's all about coming up with a major life project and bringing it closer and closer to fruition over time. Goals and projects, whether they are realized or not, lead us to feel a greater sense of satisfaction with life. Simply, pursuing projects and dreams makes us happier[69].

Many of us don't think we have much to offer the world; yet, all of us at one time or another has said, why not do it this way, or why doesn't anyone invent this, or I have a great idea for that, but oh well....I'm just me. If you look at anyone who has ever invented something, made any kind of social change, or any impact whatsoever on society, they were just that, themselves. The truth is, there's no difference between you and other amazing people other than they've taken a concrete step and you have yet to.

You might have an idea for a small business, a genius campaign concept, or a way to connect with audiences. Maybe you have a research idea, book theme, or movie pilot. It's time. Take advantage of the fact that you are new at this and if it flops you can always say, oh well, it was just a thought. But, if you don't, your great idea will go nowhere. Don't worry that it may fail, tons of ideas fail, but some are really brilliant and get taken forward. Which will yours be; do you have the courage to find out?

---

[69] *Sheldon, K. M., Abad, N., Ferguson, Y., Gunz, A., Houser-Marko, L., Nichols, C. P., & Lyubomirsky, S. (2010). Persistent pursuit of need-satisfying goals leads to increased happiness: A 6-month experimental longitudinal study. Motivation and Emotion, 34, 39–48.*

Write your idea in detail and as though you were presenting it to the CEO of a company (or publishing house, or playwright, or whoever would receive your great idea). Do it right by Googling "how to write a proposal" (film, business plan, etc.) or whatever it is you are doing.

Now, who will you pitch it to? Come up with real names and organizations. Remember, you're just planning. You can change your mind about submitting; but, push yourself a little and see how far you can get with this idea. What do you have to lose? Take your time and keep refining your idea over the course of the week. Only decide whether to submit it once you've done all the preparation, thought and planning. Then see how you feel. Good luck!

Strategy 51: It's your time!

My best possible self

Imagining our best possible self[70] helps us think about who we'd like to become, our life goals and our most cherished dreams and plan for them. Doing this activity will provide you with a feeling of control and direction and prompt you to take steps to make your best self a reality. This is an activity that you should redo many times as you will need to update your progress and determine new goals as you reach the old ones. You can do this activity on poster boards and write, paint, draw, or make a collage and elicit as much detail as possible about your best self. The activity is in two parts.

Think about who you will be when you reach your best possible self at home, work, school, with friends, and in every sphere of your life.

Part 1:
When I reach my best self, how will I look? How will my thoughts and actions be different? How will I interact with others? How will I present myself differently? Write your vision and provide as much detail as possible about the vision you have of yourself at your best.

Part 2:
Use the table to complete your best self by pulling goals from your vision and turning these into actions you can do. Fill as many boxes that apply and update these over time as you will reach them and adapt. Your steps must be realistic, reachable, and not too far away. At the end, add your resources that will help in attaining your goals.

---

[70] *Sheldon, K. M., & Lyubomirsky, S. (2006). How to increase and sustain positive emotion: The effects of expressing gratitude and visualizing best possible selves. The Journal of Positive Psychology, 1(2), 73-82.*

Part 1: My Best Self

Part 2: Best Self Goals

Family	Work	Social/Friends	Community
Health/Fitness	Education	Environment	Religion
Recreation	Finances	Travel/learning	Contribution to the world

Other

Current resources (friends, family, health, skills, smarts, money, time, etc.)

Strategy 52: Make it easy.

Nudge

You've been working on this happiness project for several weeks. That's impressive to be honest.

As we reach the end, there are still tweaks you can make to maintain your happiness and ensure it becomes a habit rather than a matter of deliberate concentration. It's called nudging[71]. It's a behavioral principle that states if you want to make something easy for people to do, make that choice easier for them to make.

For instance, if you want to eat better, ensure you have fruits and vegetables right on the counter so they are the first things you see and think of versus leaving crisps and other junk food in plain sight.

If you want to be more social, RSVP and book social events at the beginning of each month so you can't talk yourself out of them a few hours prior. You can even arrange for friends to come and collect you so it's harder to cancel.

If you want to be fitter, leave two changes of workout clothes in the car or at work so it's never an excuse and restock every weekend so you're never caught short. An extra pair of running shoes never hurts at the office either. At a minimum, you can walk every lunch hour by booking it into your schedule with an open invitation to your colleagues so you're forced to go even when you don't feel like it.

---

[71] *Vlaev, I., King, D., Dolan, P., & Darzi, A. (2016). The theory and practice of "nudging": Changing health behaviors. Public Administration Review, 76(4), 550-561.*

If you want to sleep earlier and more regularly, arrange for your internet to lock you out at 10pm, or for the lights to dim at 9pm. A pre-scheduled pop-up email at 8:45pm will also give you the heads up to shift gears and start winding down.

Get the point? Change is tough to make on your own. So make use of technology, your environment and existing habits to plan, regulate, and guide your behavior so you're not left to make these choices on your own. Humans, being what they are, will almost always opt for the junk food in plain view, but an apple would do just fine if it were there. Make sure the apple is there.

What tweaks can you make to the day to be happier, healthier, more social, active, and appreciative?

The road ahead

Congratulations! You've worked really hard and changed how you think and act. Others have noticed your changes too. You made your happiness happen all by yourself by reading, putting in effort, thinking about the ideas, and taking part in every single activity. That deserves a round of applause! Woo Hoo!!

Before you go, I have a few more words.

- Continue to partake in these strategies. You can reread this book a million times and rewrite your answers elsewhere. You'll also see how much you've changed.

- Be mindful of adaptation. While I encourage you to repeat the strategies, mix them up, do them with others, or in varied contexts so that they don't get boring and you give up.

- Don't be afraid of hard work. It's what makes us who we are. Leave mediocrity to others.

- Know that you will be laughed at or judged if it hasn't happened already. When others aren't happy, the last thing they want to be around is someone who is! It's not personal.

- You'll still be unhappy sometimes. It means you're normal. Go ahead and be unhappy, but know when enough is enough and when you decide it's time to move on from being unhappy, do it. Don't pressure yourself to be happy, it'll backfire and your unhappiness will last even longer.

This is where I leave you to live your amazing, super delicious, oversized life! Go well, live your best life! It's the only one you have...

Dr. Louise Lambert

Manufactured by Amazon.ca
Bolton, ON

28392579R00090